MW00415148

Perfectly
Imperfect

Kent Lawlor

Perfectly Imperfect

Perfectly Imperfect

To my parents who always came back to get me whenever I was left in a parking lot, and to Smith, Wynn, and Grey for making me the luckiest father in the world.

Perfectly Imperfect

Contents

Perfectly Imperfect

THE BEGINNING

My actual story starts not at the time of my birth, but just over a month later in August of 1978, in the parking lot of grocery store located in a small Long Island town just outside the looming shadows of New York City. My parents had taken the three kids to the local A&P on a quiet weekend day to do their weekly shopping for the necessities, and presumably show off their newest addition (me) to all of the elderly cackling yentas who kept close tabs on the neighborhood.

After loading everything in to the twenty-seven foot long, pale blue station wagon with faux wood grained side panels, they set off for home so that my dad could sit in his underwear on the couch and complain about how the Mets were a bunch of bums, and my mom could hide in the kitchen and pretend to care about Darryl Strawberry's batting average from afar. As the story goes, about halfway home, my mother turned to my dad and asked if he had put the baby into the car. He replied that he thought that she had, before a string of expletives and an impressive median-jumping u-turn occurred on the Long Island Expressway at 70 miles per hour. When they arrived back at the grocery store, there I sat still in the shopping cart, quiet and content, looking up at the sky and following the clouds with my eyes as they drifted lazily by. In total, it was only about 10 minutes that I was left alone in a parking lot, and to this day I'm not sure if I'm more surprised that this actually happened, or that nobody thought to call the police and report the month old baby hanging out by himself in a New York parking lot, although I

8

guess nobody really noticed because the Mets game was on and Darryl Strawberry had just struck out again.

From that point forward in my life the tone had been set. As the youngest of three kids, I was the one who was perpetually left behind, dragged along, glossed over, and often times just completely forgotten about. I grew bitter and resentful at the lack of attention that I had been given as a child. I concocted scenarios in my mind where my parents didn't love me as much as my older brother and sister, and I played the victim card continuously throughout relationships in my life, blaming the lack of success on some imagined past damage rather than who I actually was. It wasn't until my dad was diagnosed with incurable cancer riddling his entire body that I stopped to do some thinking and self-reflecting. The conclusion that I came to was a very eye opening one. It became painfully obvious…. that I

9

had been a complete and utter shithead for all of these years! Fuck.

My parents completely busted their ass to give their kids the absolute best life that they could. I held a grudge because my dad never made time to play catch in the street with me, when the reality was that he was busy working two jobs so that we would have enough money to get by and afford my mom the ability to stay home and be there before/after school. I was mad because we didn't have the money for the newest shoes/bikes/video games, but I never stopped to consider what a gift it was that my parents bought a pop-up camper and drove us across the United States THREE times, when most of my friends had never been west of Brooklyn. What. A. Completely. Selfish. Dick. My parents weren't perfect, but they worked hard to do their best, and THAT is what this is all about.

Estimates put the world's entire population, since the beginning of man, at around 102 BILLION people. That means that, mathematically speaking, there have been a complete shit ton of people who have been parents since the beginning of time, and guess what????????? Not a single ONE has done a perfect job. Let me say that again so that it can sink into your insanely evolved shoulder melon. Not a single parent, in the history of time, forever, has done a flawless job of parenting. Nobody. Ever. Anywhere. Anytime.

So what does that mean for us? It means that we're in the same bracket as any parent who has ever lived. Lincoln. Washington. Gandhi. Julius Caesar. Rerun from *What's Happening?*. That's right, you're as good, if not BETTER than all of these procreatin' sons of bitches, with no offense meant towards Rerun's mother. All too often, we start to question our abilities and intentions, but we have to remember that this is a perfection-proof profession. Nobody gets it right, we can only do our absolute best.

11

What if you took a test in 5th grade and it was somehow impossible to score 100% ? Would you be upset if you scored a 90? An 80? A 75? Remember, 100% is impossible, so we know that perfection is not an option. Or maybe a better metaphor is competing in a division III discus state tournament. You step up to the line, spin around until you're dizzy and want to throw up all of those 2-for-1 drinks you had at happy hour last night down at the Rusty Nugget, and launch that motherfucker as far as you can. There's no endzone. There's no perfect. There's just hurling that shit as far as you can and hoping you don't land it out of bounds, killing an innocent freshman engineering student who's in town for the weekend to support his nerd girlfriend who thinks the discus team just looks good on her application to a legitimate non-community college that she'd like to transfer to in the fall.

Do your best and be happy with your effort. Don't beat yourself up. We are all imperfect as human beings, it's in our nature. Those knuckleheads Adam and Eve sort of ruined it for the rest of us from the get-go. If we want to blame anyone, blame them... and division III athletics.

So why this book? You're probably saying to yourself, "what do *you* know? You got left in a shopping cart and don't know what you're talking about! You think you're so high and mighty writing a friggin' book to give *me* advice on how to raise *my* kids? You've got some nerve pencilneck!"

First off, relax. Second, my point is... you're exactly right! I don't know exactly what I'm talking about! In fact, NOBODY does! I can only give you suggestions about what worked and what didn't work for me, and maybe help you realize that you're not so out of your mind along the way. Some of these chapters you might read and want to rip out and use as an earwax candle, and to that I say GO FOR IT! My biggest advice to people who are about to have kids is, "don't listen to anyone's advice!" which I understand doesn't seem to make sense in and of itself, but you have to sort of figure it out for yourself. There's no manual. There's no 24 hour help line. You're on your own. You're going to be scared. You're going to make mistakes. You're going to have no idea what you're doing at points, but that's OK! In fact, It's better than ok, it's completely normal and par for this shitty minigolf course called parenthood, with a giant clown head at the end that sucks your soul out and never gives it back like the pink ball that you chose because it's the easiest color to find when you end up hitting it into the bushes.

Now hopefully, there will be some things in the book where you say to yourself, "Holy shit! That sounds so familiar!" or, "Wow, I never really thought of it like that," but I think the biggest takeaway from this book is that you realize that you're not alone. You're part of a large and distinguished group called *Everyone Who Has Ever Had Kids, Literally Ever.* Suddenly it's not so scary when you realize that the

14

things that you're feeling have been felt billions of times over the course of thousands of years.

Who knows, maybe there was a time when even Mr. and Mrs. Brachiosaurus felt guilty about how a t-rex ripped their baby's fucking face off and had it for brunch with some Mesozoic mimosas. I bet they felt like total reptilian failures. But did they roll over into a tar pit and give up? Well, maybe. But maybe not! Maybe they soldiered on and birthed the baby brachiosaurus who was the first to become friends with the pteranodons, motivating them to grow some feathers and become some modern-day bird faced motherfreakers! Fast forward a few million years and next thing you know, we've got a giant yellow bird staring in his own tv show teaching our kids how to read on some run down block in, in what I presume is the Bronx, because there's green guys living in garbage cans and meth-fueled vampires walking around in the daytime obsessing over counting grams and kilos. Are you following where I'm going? Me neither.

The beauty of the following chapters is that none of them are meant to be followed word for word. This isn't a how-to book. In fact, this is a who-fucking-knows book. It's a book to make you think, laugh, reflect, realize, and enjoy, all while hopefully coming to the conclusion that you don't have to be perfect. No parent is perfect. No kid is perfect. So, don't hold yourself to perfect standards. You're completely kicking ass, and you're doing a great job. Think about this... the entire reason why you're stressing over whether you're doing a "good job" or not is actually because you're a good parent. You think a shitty parent is really going to expend the energy to worry about whether or not they're doing a good job? The answer is no. They're short-sighted and only think about themselves. You're concerned about your child. You're concerned about your role as a parent. THAT, without any other outside qualifying factors proves that you're a good parent. You care. You reflect. You think. That's what it's about. Do your best, you child-raising motherfucker you, and don't let anyone question your choices... because you know your child the better than anyone else on the planet, and you're going to do what's right for them. THAT is what makes you a real parent and not some bum like a third string relief pitcher for the 1978 Mets.

Perfectly Imperfect

TONE

You've had those days. Those days were nothing comes easy and everything seems to go wrong and continue going wrong. After waking up late because your alarm didn't go off, you don't have time for your morning coffee ritual, your toast gets burnt, everyone seems to be taking a nice relaxing Sunday drive on the way to work even though it isn't Sunday, your boss surprises you with a spreadsheet that absolutely needs to be done by the end of the day or the world might collapse in on itself, the office printer is obviously plotting against you, and to top it off you've got on two different shoes and just realized that you may or may not have left the kitchen sink

19

running. By the end of the day you feel like if anything else even slightly goes wrong, you're committed to selling all of your worldly possessions, buying thirty pounds of ostrich jerky, and going to live in the forest where you can talk to a stump and nobody will bother you.

The truth of this is that any of those events, taken individually, are really not that much of an issue. Ok, maybe the kitchen sink running all day, but otherwise, the rest are just small inconveniences that have become compounded and part of the greater shit-storm. *This* is how tone works, and it was one of the most important revelations for me as a parent. By being mindful of things on an individual scale, it's much easier to keep from getting overwhelmed and wrapped up in ineffective communication. It is not only what you are actually saying to your child, but also the feeling behind it and the way that it is presented to them. The tone you have with your children can improve the overall mood of the house, your child's happiness, and your sanity, or it can fuel a fire until it burns wildly out of control without regard for anyone in its path. Tone is the one thing that can be so easy to do with a bit of mindfulness, paying off in dividends. It can be the difference between quiet calm, and a swirling vortex of ever-increasing volume and emotion that leaves relationships strained and pants peed.

Young children are very much like the out of control drunken roommate that you lived with in college. The one who was loud and quite often obnoxious, would babble incessantly, leave clothing strewn all over the house, never do dishes, and sometimes pee in their closet, but in the end, we are responsible for molding these tiny humans into contributing members of society. So, think back to your days of reckless debauchery, how did we best communicate with our out of control friend who couldn't hold their liquor? By using a quiet, relaxed, and calming tone. Reverse psychology at its most gloriously triumphant. Much like your college roommate, when your child decides that it's time to try to ride the dog around the living room or play frisbee golf with their plate of macaroni and cheese, the most effective way to correct their behavior is with a quiet, relaxed tone. It seems unnatural at first, because they're being a savage and carrying on like its Mardi Gras and beads are in short supply, but it will work. Be persistent. Don't let the turkeys get you down. When you start speaking in a quiet voice, they will eventually start to listen. Raising your voice has the opposite effect.

Think about it, even though we like to think that we're so intelligent and advanced, humans are actually quite primitive creatures. We function optimally when we are in a relaxed, low-stress state. Millions of years ago cavemen and cavewomen relied heavily on their senses and were always aware of impending doom that might come at any moment in the form of an ornery pterodactyl or near-sighted mammoth. When the sabretooth tiger started sniffing around the campfire looking for brunch, heartbeats began to elevate, brain neurons began to fire, and the fight-or-flight instinct kicked into effect. Now, I'm not comparing your situation to Zog the caveman, and you to a sabretooth tiger who wants to snack on the endocrine system of your unsuspecting prey, but it's certainly related.

When a child hears a sudden, loud, commanding voice, their first reaction is that heartrates go up, and they experience a miniature feeling of fight-or-flight in response to perceived danger. They're not preparing to fight in the sense of hurling spears at you, but they will protect themselves in the way that they know how, which is usually to raise their own voice and become defiant. Kids have *reasons* for their behavior. They aren't just throwing that fit because it's a personal thing and they want to intentionally piss *you* off, it's for another reason that unfortunately is usually not easy to decipher, especially as they lay screaming on the floor of the home improvement aisle of Target. It might be a response to stress, it might be self-protection, it might be the lack of appropriate communication skills, but there IS a reason. In turn, if the chaos and defiance causes *your* heartrate, blood pressure, and volume to increase, they will feed off of it like parasitic leeches and suck out your soul through a straw, and not a regular straw, one of those thin coffee stirrer straws to make it extra-long and excruciating, and use that power to form into a supreme force like Voltron and destroy anything in their path. I digress. TONE. Tone! It takes some getting used to, it really does, and you need to consciously make it a habit to speak in a relaxed state at all times so that it comes naturally when shit hits the metaphorical fan with your kids. You must become a Zen master, a tree that bends in the wind but does not break in the storm, a plankton that floats with the ebbs and tides of the sea, or a snowflake that settles cozily beneath the crushing weight of those above.

When it does finally become a habit, your whole demeanor will change. You will find yourself more relaxed on a regular basis, and better prepared when the cavemen begin to get restless. It will permeate your life, and you'll find that the things that usually made you want to flee out of a third story window will roll off your back like droplets off the majestic surfacing humpback. You will notice it, people around you will notice it, and most importantly your children will notice it.

Author Peggy O'Mara said that, "the way we talk to our children becomes their inner voice." If we aim to provide loving guidance rather than commanding without feeling, we are instilling our children with the qualities of compassion, understanding, and patience that will be solidified deep within their character for their entire life.

Think about how you get your child's attention when you want them to listen? Do you yell? Do you find yourself repeating their names over and over like you're not even speaking the same language as them? My guess is probably both, depending on the situation, and guess what, that's a struggle that every parent has been through, even if they don't admit it.

There ARE times when calling their name in a sudden, loud, somewhat scary way is appropriate. I'm not saying that you should *never* raise your voice, but I am saying that it should be withheld for only certain situations, such as when there is actual danger. If your child is running towards the street with no clue that a school bus full of nuns is hurtling towards them, then yes, please get their attention as loudly and as quickly as possible. When kids hear their voice like that, most times they freeze and pants peeing occurs, but I'd rather clean up some pee pants than an entire busload of sisters, got me?

Right now you might be saying to yourself, "ok, sounds legit, but how do I actually go about doing this?" The good news is that it's not necessarily hard. It's not like you have to travel to a distant village in Nepal and consult the oracle who will then send you on a quest to recover the golden hawk's feather from the top of the snow covered peak so that you can prove yourself worthy. No. It's much simpler than that. In fact, it only takes some self-reflection and consciousness in the following areas:

1) **Proximity:** In my experience, the closer I am to a child, the more likely they are to listen. In a classroom setting, many times the teacher only needs to make a slight adjustment to where they are physically standing in order to change the level of attention of a student or students. Think about it in terms of your own work. When one of your eight bosses are hovering

27

around your cubicle for no apparent reason, you at least heighten your level of awareness and possibly even open up a spreadsheet over the current game of solitaire that you're playing on your computer. The same thing happens when you speak with a child. If you're on the other side of the house and yell over that you need them to clean up their toys, the seriousness of the message will be lost over the distance. Instead, move closer to your child to make sure that you have eye contact, and express to them what you need.

2) **Contact:** When you are close to your child, begin by making contact through a light touch on the shoulder or arm. This subtle touch signals to your child that you are both connected, and that what you are

about to say is important. Note: you are not *grabbing* the child, because that would again put them immediately into the fight-or-flight state of mind, and cause tensions to rise which prevents effective communication. I have also found that if you keep your connection and leave your hand on their shoulder throughout your instructions, children are much more likely to hear the entire message, and removal of the connection will act as a signal to begin whatever it is that you need them to do.

3) **Level:** Bending down or kneeling at the child's level puts them in a more comfortable state because they are not facing a physically imposing being, which will bring down their guard and make them more likely to listen. There are

numerous studies that explore the relationship between height and perceived intimidation, with most suggesting that people who are nearest to your height are least intimidating and perceived as most trustworthy.

4) **Message:** Although I fully believe that *how* you say something is much more important than *what* you say, I also believe that the *what* is extremely important too. Be sure that your message is short, to the point, and understandable. It's easy to start going into a thirty-minute dissertation about the financial, developmental, and ethical reasons why your child should eat their cereal, but is that message being clearly communicated, or is it just a vehicle for you to blow off steam and get some things off your chest? Communicating what you

need, and a very short explanation of *why* you need it, resonates much deeper with a child than a 4500-word essay. "I need you to finish your breakfast so that we can get dressed for school" makes much more sense to a three year old than, "Would you please just eat your cereal because I go out of my way to go to the one store that sells this cereal because I know you like it, and you're not even eating it! We have to be out the door in twenty minutes because mommy has another pointless meeting with her pathetic boss, and if you're not eating then we're probably going to hit traffic all the way to school and then we're going to sit in the carline with all those fake bitchy moms in their Land Rovers who have nothing better to do than just go to the gym, or actually just wear their yoga pants like a badge of honor and pretend like they

31

go to the gym. I've been eating shakes for lunch for months and I still can't lose these love handles that YOU gave me. Damnit, we need to go!"

5) **Monitor:** Although I'd like to tell you that we can tell a child something once and it will get done exactly how we wanted and in a timely manner, that's just simply not the case. Kids have a wonderful gift for finding a way to mess things up, but usually it's due to a lack of experience or clarity, and not just because they're savages and like to make everything difficult... although I'm not completely ruling that out either. I once asked my four-year-old son to put his shoes away because they had been in the living room for days, but the next morning they weren't where we usually put the shoes and we were running late for

school. Frustrated, I went on a tirade about being responsible, paying attention, and doing what I ask him to do, but he just stared at me obviously confused. He told me that he had, in fact, put his shoes away when I told him to, so with much exasperation I asked him to go get them wherever they might be. Without hesitation, he walked directly into the kitchen, opened the refrigerator, and retrieved his missing shoes from behind a bottle of mayonnaise. Unsure of whether to be happy that he actually did know where the shoes were, mad because they were not put away correctly in the first place, or concerned for his mental well-being because he was obviously confused as to the actual purpose of a refrigerator, it was in that moment that I realized that in his mind he was doing exactly what I had

33

asked. Now, with the importance of monitoring in mind, I also want to play devil's advocate and caution you that following *too* closely can also be a negative thing. I'm sure you've heard the term "helicopter parent" referring to those who are always within arm's reach of their children, constantly instilling fear by pointing out every bad scenario that could play out. "Be careful!" "Don't do that!" "You'll shoot your eye out!" A child needs some degree of autonomy to be able to explore life and come to their own conclusions. Yes, sometimes those conclusions come in the form of painful lessons, but the experience gained is priceless. As parents we must try to walk the tightrope somewhere between keeping our children sheltered from the world and giving them too much free reign like they were the Lord of the Flies.

LET GO

Something magical happens to most kids towards the end of high school. Maybe it's earlier for some I'm not sure, but for me, being the shy artsy-shartsy kid that I was, it was during my senior year. With the newfound freedom that came with a driver's license and the occasional use of my mom's super sweet two-tone grey van with maroon faux-leather interior and tinted front bug deflector, mixed with the nervous excitement of knowing that college was just a few short months away (holy shit I'll be able to stay up all night, leave my underwear on the floor, eat waffles for dinner, and maybe even... gasp... talk to girls?! Ok, maybe that's getting ahead of myself, but waffles for sure) I felt like I was finally becoming something that partially resembled an adult.

The summer before heading off to college out of state, it felt as though Bryan Adams was singing about my life, except less Canadian. My friends and I would spend hours washing our cars before cruising around town looking for but somehow never finding girls, attend countless backyard parties at the home of whoever's parents were away that weekend, climb up to the roof and lay out in the pursuit of the perfect tan (this was New York after all, and even though nobody we knew had a pool, being tan was of utmost importance,) and listen to the music that still to this day brings me right back to that summer and the smell of that one girl's hair.

Most nights, after meticulously preening and practicing my lethal finger guns in the mirror, one of my friends would pull up in front of the house, announcing their arrival from down the street with monstrous bass that vibrated three square blocks like an electric toothbrush, emanating from a vehicle that was more suited to be featured as an extra in *The Fast and the Furious Part 73: Knuckehead's Return,* than belonging to a kid who sweeps the floor of the local bagel store for minimum wage. Hearing the call, I would bound towards the door like a parched gazelle during the rainy season, trying to make a clean getaway before my parents started giving me the third degree about who I was going out with, where I was going, who was going to be there, and why was there a towel on the roof. As I hurried out and mumbled my goodbyes to my parents who were usually on the couch talking about how Alex Trebek never ages, my mom would always look up and casually say the same thing every time… "be careful, and….. wake me when you get home."

Most of those times, I would get home late after a night of doing what teenagers do, including but not limited to underage drinking, failing to obey traffic laws, occasional destruction of property, habitual disorderly conduct, and all-around portrayal of poor decision making. (In other words, some good old-fashioned fun.) My friends would dump me on the front lawn and peel off into the darkness, taking out mailboxes, fire hydrants, and anyone unlucky and/or dumb enough to be going for an early morning run. After trying every key 17 times, I would go into stealth mode and attempt to sneak my way upstairs to let my parents know that I was home, and not at all completely smashed out of my underage gourd.

In complete darkness, I felt like I was a jaguar hunting its prey through the dense jungle, aware of every breath, footstep, and placement of crunchy sticks in the undergrowth that would possibly compromise my position. I was an anaconda silently slipping through the murky water of the everglades, an owl alighting from the forest canopy to pick off an unsuspecting mouse, or a satellite crossing the nighttime sky with only a small light announcing its presence from miles above the earth. When I was finally in position at the side of the bed, I would gently tap my mom's foot until I heard her stir, and I would hold my breath (so that she wouldn't be hit with the gasoline-like fumes left behind by whatever I had been pouring into my gaping head that night) and quietly let her know that I was home safe, to which she would often reply something to the effect of, "I know, I heard you fall up the stairs." Thinking I was as slick as an Exxon Valdez waterfowl, I would quickly retreat to my room where I could pray away all of my bad sins and promise God that I was absolutely never drinking again if he would just have mercy and make my room stop spinning like when you would put your ruler on the tip of your pencil and pretend to be a helicopter in third grade.

I never thought much of my parent's words and actions before I left the house all those nights, but I now realize that was so much more than just cordiality. It was one of the most loving things that a parent could say and do. It was my mom saying that she loved me, that she trusted everything would turn out alright, and that I would come back to her safely. It was the act of letting go, and now that I am a parent, I see that it is one of the most difficult, but at the same time most important, things that we must learn to do.

Despite our own fear of the unknown, we must realize that we can only do so much for our children, and the rest they must do on their own. We, as parents, do the absolute best that we can do from the moment our child is born, and we instill along the way all the values and beliefs that we find important, but in the end our children will grow to be individuals.

They will make their own decisions, follow what they think is important, chase what makes them happy, and find joy and a lot of pain along the way. We can hope that they will make good choices, and not be hurt, but there comes a time when the only right thing for a parent to do is to let go and trust. Trust that they have heard, and truly listened to what we have told them. Trust that we have set a good example for them to follow. Trust that there is a higher power out there somewhere looking over them. Trust that everything is, somehow, going to be alright.

When it comes to letting go, there's good news, and there's bad news. The bad news is that the act of stepping back, letting go, and trusting that everything will be fine goes against every basic prehistoric parenting instinct. Thousands of years ago, Zog the Caveman didn't just simply trust that his newborn child would be fine by themselves, napping on a rock somewhere while he went out and hunted for some delicious gluten free mammoth rump. If that was the case, he probably would've returned to find out that some near-sighted pachycephalosaurus wasn't watching where he was going and gave Zog Jr. the old flaming bag of poop on the porch treatment if you know what I mean. With the lack of quality dino optometrists around during the Mesozoic era (I mean, who could afford medical school on a caveman salary, am I right?) the number of instances of "Zog stomping" could have become an epidemic if cave-babies were just being left around all willy-nilly, which would've changed the course of human population and history as we know it!

Lucky for us, Zog listened to his instincts and wasn't so quick to let go, but for us super modernized and not at all giant foreheady people, that shit is hard! We could worry ourselves to death if we focused all our time on what could possibly go wrong. The act of creating a healthy human being that starts from a single cell, grows in another human beings' body, is birthed, and then continues to grow physically and intellectually into a full-sized person capable of doing things like developing the world's first waterproof burrito is, in my opinion, nothing short of a miracle.

An infinite array of things can go wrong at any stage along the way, so how could we *possibly* just trust that it'll all going to somehow turn out alright?!

Before you start overthinking this and consider channeling your inner Zog, let me get to the good news, which is that the stakes aren't nearly as high as it was for Mr. Cromagnon. If you let go and allow your child to experience challenge and/or difficulty, the worst that is going to happen is *not* that they are going to end up as Jurassic fertilizer, it is only going to result in growth. Possibly failure, but ultimately growth.

If you remind your child once to study for their spelling test and they don't, it might result in a failing grade and a bit of upset, but what they *gain* from it is much more important. Your child will connect the lack of preparation with failure and may do better the next time to avoid these unwanted feelings. By the time they are more grown up, and the stakes become a bit larger (with possible negative consequences being losing jobs, failed relationships, being arrested, etc.) they will already have experience in how to deal with difficulty and can plan ahead. In short, by facing adversity early on, your child will be more prepared to face the tough times that life will almost certainly throw at them.

In the past few years, a new term has become increasingly common to describe parents who are overprotective and discourage a child's independence by becoming overly involved. Ask any teacher you know, and they'll have stories ranging from adults who do their kid's homework for them, to parents who call school to defend their child's poor behavior and place blame on anyone and everyone else. (Well yes, I understand that my son stabbed another child in the ear with a pencil, but *why* are these children being given such sharp writing utensils to begin with? It could've been prevented! My child is the real victim here! This is unacceptable!!) The term that I'm talking about, is "helicopter parent." These

46

are the parents that have difficulty, or have consciously made the decision, to *not* let go. Rather than letting a child have experiences that will build upon their character, helicopter parents are convinced that if they are involved in absolutely every aspect of their child's life, they can steer their child in the right direction (or, at least *their* idea of what the right direction is.)

In extreme cases, helicopter parents are sometimes referred to as "bulldozer parents," meaning that they have made it their sole mission in life to completely remove any obstacles so that their kids have a life that is completely devoid of difficulty. While the basic principle of hovering or bulldozing comes from a place of love and concern for their children, what these parents actually help create is a child who lacks problem solving skills, a sense of personal accomplishment, independence, self-esteem, and life skills. This form of parent also builds anxiety, and an unrealistic sense of entitlement.

47

Educator, author, and philosopher Maria Montessori was quoted as saying, "Never help a child with a task at which he feels like he can succeed." Would it be quicker and easier to tie your second graders shoes every before school? Absolutely. Especially when you still need to pack 3 lunches, do your hair, sign field trip permission slips, feed the cat, start the laundry, remove the Lego block from the bottom or your foot, and locate underwear for your three-year-old who is currently running around the house naked with a spaghetti strainer on her head. But, would your second grader ever learn how to tie his shoes? Would he feel the sense of accomplishment and pride in doing it himself? Would he learn how to persevere when a task became difficult?

Now to be clear, I'm not suggesting that parents sit back and let their children completely flounder like a, well, a flounder out of water. Obviously, the main job of a parent is to help them learn how to be responsible, successful, good people, but the operative words there are *help* and *learn*. It doesn't help our children if we're always swooping in to do things for them, and they certainly won't learn anything other than that they don't have to put much effort into anything at all because someone is just going to pat them on the head, give them a lollipop, and make it all better in the end. *Those* kids are the weak ones. *Those* are the ones who show no grit. *Those* are the ones who make you want to drown yourself in the punchbowl when you get stuck talking to them at your spouse's office Christmas party.

It may seem like a paradox to let your kids fail, but in truth it is exactly what makes you a good parent. Let them learn, let them experience, let them grow... they will become stronger because you let go.

Perfectly Imperfect

LAUGH

My son, like many young children, was a proud amateur nudist (are there professional nudists? Remind me to Google that later.) Two-year olds rarely understand that finer points of social norms and therefore find it completely acceptable to gallivant around house sans clothes, proudly showing off their butts like a mandrill baboon, to anyone up to and including the mailman, pizza delivery girl, and Janice from your book club with the weak heart.

One afternoon, he was playing quietly in his room when I heard a noise that can only be described as part horrified scream, part cry, and part coyote getting its foot stuck in one of those metal hunting traps. I bolted into his room to find him standing there with a shocked expression on his face, no clothes on, and a significant amount of shit rolling slowly down his leg. We locked eyes and time stood still for a moment until, thinking he would be in trouble, he ran and hid in his closet trailing excrement and slamming the sliding doors shut on the tracks behind him.

After taking a moment to process and assess the situation, I immediately began on damage control. I calmly opened the sliding door and carefully transferred my son down the hall to the bath like I was removing an isotope from the inner sanctum of Chernobyl. After bathing the biohazard and sanitizing the entire bathroom, my attention turned to cleaning up the carnage in his room which looked like the first day of the Exxon Valdez spill minus the waterfowl and random harbor seal.

The initial cleanup, although gross, wasn't all too bad. Nothing that some bleach, a hazmat suit, and an industrial grade sandblaster couldn't take care of. More than an hour passed after the cleanup was complete, but still a pungent odor permeated the entire upstairs, causing eyes to tear up and birds to fall lifeless from the trees outside. A search party was formed, and it was soon discovered that there was a significant amount of, what scientists call dookie, caked INTO the tracks of the sliding closet door. Removal of said dookie required full removal of two closet doors, a bulk supply of q-tips, one high-powered wet-vac, 37 rolls of paper towels, and the better part of a Sunday afternoon.

Now, at this point in our saga, my two options were to freak out and burn the entire house down in a rage, or.... to laugh. I took a moment to sit back and consider the absurdity of the situation and laugh at the story that I would be able to tell, someday, to you. This is just one small example. Chances are, you will have hundreds if not thousands of these moments throughout the course of parenthood where you will

53

look up to the heavens and ask yourself, "why me?" It is in these trying times, when you want to give up and commit the ancient Japanese suicide ritual of seppuku, that you need to try to find the humor in the situation and just laugh. Realize that shit happens, often literally, and sometimes in the tracks of a sliding closet door.

KEEP GOING

As you probably have already figured out, being a parent, and especially being a parent to the best of your abilities, is really friggin hard. I'm talking ping-pong ball into the tiny fishbowl at the carnival hard, except you're throwing a Volkswagen, and it's on fire, while your mortal enemy is standing behind you relentlessly making fun of your high school yearbook picture because you look like a 30-year-old Scottish lesbian. Just me? Well anyway, that kind of hard.

There will be just as many, if not more, hard/frustrating/infuriating times as there will be happy times, but our job as parents is to keep going and never stop being a parent. This shit isn't like owning a goldfish. We can't just feed the thing once or twice a week, flush it down the toilet when it dies a month later, and then replace it with a similar one so that our neighbors don't too many questions. It's a commitment. A grind. A marathon. Nay, a permanent ultra-marathon through the desert in July with gila monsters nipping at our heels and spitting cobras, well, spitting. It doesn't stop. Like it or not, you're in it for the long haul.

There have been countless studies that attempted to measure the level of happiness of both parents and non-parents, with mixed and often times conflicting results. Several of these concluded that while adults with children are often more stressed and "unhappy" on a day-to-day basis, they are eventually happier with the overall quality of their life when it comes to an end. In short, parenting is really friggin hard, and you might question your sanity every day, but in the end, you'll be happy you did it. As I mentioned before, there's going to be a LOT of trying times, but the good times will actually be amazing. Think about the first time your child looked at you and smiled. Think about their little laugh when they were learning how to roll over. Think about how they used to lay in your arms and look up at you with nothing but love in their eyes. See that? You're smiling. And just for a moment, you forgot about that one time that they shit on the carpet and the dog walked through it, tracking it around the house. The trying times pass. The good times, no matter how small, will stay with you forever.

One of my favorite biographies is that of Soichiro Honda, who is the founder of the Honda Motor Company. Beginning from a wooden shack making bicycles, Honda rose to be one of the most recognizable names in the automotive industry, but not without adversity which included his factory being destroyed TWICE, once by a U.S. WWII bomber and again by the 1945 Mikawa earthquake.

Metaphorically, it was like Honda had dreams of going out for a beautiful steak dinner at a 5-star restaurant, but when he got there, he was given the shittiest seat in the house, and then served a large steaming shit sandwich. When he sent it back, the waiter returned with an undercooked shit steak and a side of shit-n-chips. Honda complained, which resulted in the manager shit slapping him, and shitting in his already shitty lemon water. I forgot where I was going with this metaphor, but I assure you, he went through a lot of shit.

At any point, a normal person would've said eff this and gone out and gotten an entry level position at a go-cart track, in hopes of working his/her way up and one day becoming chief flag waver... but not Honda. Fuck no. He kept going. He knew what he had to do, and he didn't let the difficulties turn him away from what he felt was right.

So, what the hell does he have to do with your kids? Well, I'll tell you. Just when you think everything is going well, your kids are going to metaphorically bomb your factory or shit in your lemon water. They are going to do something that shocks and confuses you. They are going to pierce their nose, drop out of college without talking to you first, move to Germany with their unemployed boyfriend, or start listening to rappers whose names start with Lil'.

Before you freak out and move to an iceberg adrift in the Indian Ocean, remember that they are going to sometimes make decisions that you might not agree with. Our job is to remain supportive, express our concerns, but not force our opinions. Remember when you wanted to run away from home? Remember that time when you snuck out to meet that boy from your algebra class? Remember when you listened to, gasp, Hanson?! A natural part of growing up is finding your own path. I did it, you did it, and your kids will do it. Don't give up on them no matter how hair-brained their path is, they are going to do it regardless of what you say, and they will most likely grow past it and come back to you if you support them. If you're really lucky, maybe they'll even come cheer you on when you're running your ultra-marathon.

FORGIVE YOURSELF

I was seven years old, sitting in front of the large brown cabinet tv with the rotary channel dial, eating three-month-old Boo Berry Crunch cereal and watching Batman. It wasn't the modern Batman, with the cool black molded suit serving justice throughout a brooding and broken city, it was the original Adam West series where it's a bunch of guys wearing brightly colored tights and taking extremely... long... and unnecessary... pauses... for dramatic effect.

Our hero was valiantly trying to decipher The Riddler's clues and save The Boy Wonder, when I came out of my boob-tube induced trance long enough to realize that there had been something passing in front of my vision at a high rate of speed, repeatedly for the last several minutes. Using my own bat-like detective skills, I quickly came to the conclusion that my mother had been chasing my sister around the circle that connected the living room and the kitchen, with a raised wooden spoon, threatening to end her life by way of ladling. Curses spewed from my mom's mouth that would've made The Penguin squawk in time with a colorfully animated KA-POW, as they tore past me like a squirrel with its nuts on fire (see what I did there?) The younger prey eventually managed to tire its pursuer, and I was able to piece together through many expletives and raised voices, that the entire episode centered around my sister not wanting to go to school that day. My shock wasn't that my sister wanted to stay home, that was an everyday occurrence between grades four and six, nor was it with my mother being annoyed, it was with the heightened *level* to which this regular conflict had risen to that morning. There was only one explanation. My mom had finally lost it.

"Losing it" is something that we all have done and will no doubt do again sometime in the future. It is a simple fact of life. Some days, things that are usually not a big deal, for one reason or another, become compounded, and your head explodes like it's the second coming of Mt. Vesuvius.

Even the most zen yoga master goes through times when punching an infant in the neck seems like a totally appropriate response to not being able to find their keys. The fact of the matter is that you're human (I believe) and you have those confusing and often times annoying things called emotions. Barring serial killers, roid ragers, and children's birthday party mimes, most of us have gotten pretty good at controlling most of our emotions and existing as functioning members of society without freaking out like Michael Douglas in Falling Down. The reality though, is that sometimes we all lose it at some point, the only thing that differs might be the extent to which we lose it.

On average, these episodes are usually brief, explosive, and if they are directed at or in the proximity of our children, come with a large dose of post-freak out parent guilt after you realize what you just said or did. *I can't believe I just called my 2 year old a "ratchet ass pompous womp."* Should we think or say these things? Probably not. Are they accurate? Almost definitely.

Nobody *wants* to call our kid a twatwaffle, but sometimes that's the only word we can use to accurately communicate our feelings. I'm sure if you look in a thesaurus there are dozens of more acceptable synonyms for twatwaffle, but who's got the time to thumb through all the way to the Ts and ruminate on the effectiveness of each word? Not me. Not when my daughter is pouring chocolate syrup into her underwear drawer because her toothbrush wasn't talking back to her. If we mentally beat ourselves up over every single time we were unable to bite our tongue or handle a situation with the grace of the Queen of England, we would end up spending all of our time laying on the floor of the bathroom crying into a wine and tear stained bathmat, instead of doing what we need to do, which is forgiving ourselves and continuing on with life. We all make mistakes. We say things we shouldn't. We sometimes lose it no matter how hard we try. It doesn't make you a bad person, it makes you human. Make a mental note and think of how we could've handled the situation a bit better next time, and put it in the past. Tomorrow will be another day.

Dwelling in the past and replaying scenarios in your mind, kicking yourself for how you reacted, not only negatively effects your mental state, but also sets you up for more difficult situations. If you're feeling badly about how you reacted, you might give in on something that you might usually not, to sort of settle the score in your mind. This causes confusion in your child, who now doesn't know what to expect the next time they want something / break something / do something / whatever something. The child then feels anxiety, often causing them to act out, which can potentially start the entire scenario over again, careening off the cliff like Thelma and Louise in that movie who's name I can't quite come up with at the moment. But I digress.

To make a long story shorter, don't worry about the one or two (hundred) times you lose it. Instead, think of how incredible of a parent you are every day. You got your kids to school today? You're awesome! You cooked a somewhat healthy dinner that they actually ate? You're amazing! You made sure all of your kids had pants on before they left the house this morning? Holy shit, you're killing this effing parenting thing! Nobody went to the hospital/insane asylum/morgue today? What the fuck?! Are you some sort of parenting guru that has descended from the Tibetan mountain range?! If this were an 80's movie about bmx bikes, everyone would be calling you radical! Yes, YOU. Imperfectly PERFECT in every sense of the word. Go on with your bad self.

EXPECT

In October of 1763, the famed French statesman and military leader Napoleon Bonaparte was fully engaged in leading his loyal army against the rebels during the deadly and little-known Second Baguette War, when news came to him that he would be having his first son. Although the bloody battle raged on, Napoleon was consumed with the thoughts of how the heir would take his rightful place alongside him in the halls of historical history stuff. He was overcome with pride.

Upon news of the birth, the country rejoiced in knowing that the world would have its next military genius who would continue the legacy set forth by his esteemed father. During a childhood of royal grooming, it came time for the boy to be fully immersed in the military lifestyle so that he could fulfill his destiny and be seated at the right hand of his father. With only hours before the ceremony to initiate him into the ranks of the legion, the boy went to see his father in the general's quarters. With tears in his eyes and a heavy heart, the boy hesitantly explained that he did not want to follow in his father's footsteps. He did not want to command troops to crush opposing armies and march across distant lands, gobbling up all that lay in their path in the name of the king, destroying all those who would not bow to their new sire. He had no desire to prove himself in war, gaze upon the blood-soaked battlefields, or breath in the smoke rising from the smoldering remains of the opposition. There was no armor that would ever protect the feelings in his heart, and no sword that would strike down enemies of his dreams. What he wanted to do, was dance. He wanted to feel the wind through his hair as he soared, leotardedly, across the stage, feeling the adulation of the crowd and the cheers that pumped blood through his veins like a misdirected catheter.

As the words came forth from his son, the great general Napoleon sat in silence. His dreams of conquering Europe with his son by his side were dashed against the rocks of the pounding ocean of fatherhood. The boy sat quietly, expecting to be cast away in disappointment, the shame and disappointment of an entire empire. At last, Napoleon spoke. He told his son, softly, that he was proud of him. He said to the boy that he would forever love him unconditionally, but that he must make one promise. Napoleon, looking in the eyes of his son, told him that if it was truly his dream in life to dance, that he must be the best God damned dancer there ever was. That boy grew up to be none other than George Michael. Fucking incredible.

71

Now, although this story is completely fabricated and untrue, it does stand to prove one important point. Whatever direction our children take in life, parents need to set high expectations. As mentioned in previous chapters, it's important for a child to be able to follow their own unique path in life. Chances are, it won't be the path that we had envisioned for them, but they are their own living organism and must find their own way. Whatever that way is, parents should support them and help them become the best that they can be. Sounds easy enough, but it may be more of a tightrope that it seems at first thought.

All children should be held to high standards. We should expect that our children will be genuinely good people, who contribute positively to society, and only get drunk and blackout at most once or twice a week when they are at or above the legal age to consume alcoholic beverages. That's a minimum. Children should be expected to hold strong values.

They should understand and practice respect, compassion, humility, dependability, grit, patience, honesty, courage, adaptability, self-control, kindness, curiosity, optimism, gratitude, and leadership. They should be expected to use their brain, but to follow their heart.

The good news is that your child can easily learn these critical character traits through watching you. The bad news is that it takes work, mindfulness, and consistency. One of the earliest forms of learning becomes evident when a child begins to mimic the world around them. From replicating repeated sounds to copying simple movements, children learn best by following the cues of what they see and hear. Whatever we do, whether we know it or not, is consumed by the child and put into a mental filing system as "normal behavior." They figure, well hey, the big person is doing this, and they've made it that far in life, so I should probably be doing that too. We must become the kind of person who we want our son or daughter to be. Notice I said the "kind of person," because there's going to be some variation no matter what you do. You can't, and nor should you even try to, force someone to be who *you* want them to be.

COMPARISON

They're everywhere. Even if you don't know them, they're there. Those families. The ones who drive Mercedes rather than minivans. The ones who are constantly dressed to the nines rather than the twos. The ones who have the kids who are in the gifted class, play concert violin, are on the junior Olympic soccer team, and never have a stain on their impeccably creased khakis, while your child still thinks that there's a magical man inside the toaster who paints the bread brown and sprays it with "burny smelly spray."

75

How do they do it? How are they so... together? Why does it seem so effortless for them to be the Sears catalogue family, always smiling and looking happy while the breeze gently kisses the perfect wisp of hair that is in no way similar to the rats nest ponytail that you're sporting because your three year old decided that the best time to paint the wall with syrup was the exact moment that you stepped into the shower this morning. Would you like their secret? Would you like to know how you too can have the perfect family? Yes? Ok, here it is. Are you ready? Write this down. Their secret is... (suspense suspense suspense)... it's all bullshit. Seriously. It's all a façade, which by the way I'm pretty sure is French for "that shit don't exist." Smoke and mirrors, like when Bruce Lee was trying to fight Han in the Hall of Mirrors at the end of *Enter the Dragon*, but then he hears, "destroy the image and you will break the enemy." Yeah, same thing, except with less roundhouse kicks to the jugular. Everyone who seems

76

to have the perfect situation or even "have it together at all times" is simply good at projecting an image, while behind closed doors things are often way different than they seem. As a teacher I've seen this a hundred times. It's the child who always has the new clothes and is picked up in the fanciest cars that are often times the biggest mess. That's not to say that material things equal messed up kids, not at all, but there are many parents who are so consumed with the outward image of the family, that the interior foundation is crumbling. We can't compare ourselves to anyone else because what is important to one person/family, is often completely unimportant to another. Would you rather live in the house with the shiny new paint on the outside and a crumbling interior, or the one without much curb appeal, but what it lacks in looks it makes up with a strong foundation and cozy warmth? I know which one I'd pick.

Growing up, I lived in a lower/middle class neighborhood on Long Island, not far outside the boundary of New York City. At the time it was much like, as comedian Jim Brueur put it, "Little Rascals meets Goodfellas" with half the neighborhood being working class families doing what they could to get by, and the other half being newly transplanted families who moved out from the city to live the "quiet" life. Among all my friends who were 100% off the boat and most likely connected Italian, I was the lone Irish kid with a name that didn't fit in with the standard Vinnys, Nickys, Michaelangelos, and Dinos. The families who had been there since I was a kid had modest houses, multiple jobs, and cars that got them from A to B, while the families that came later lived down by the Long Island Sound, in large houses with white carpeted rooms that you weren't allowed to set foot in, drove whale-like Cadillacs, and had heartbreakingly beautiful daughters with exotic names like Rosemary and Carmela. The thing was, at

78

the end of the day, if I had to do it all over again, I would want to be exactly where I was, with the parents who laid awake at night thinking about where the next mortgage payment was going to come from, but who loved their kids unconditionally, taught them how to be good people, and wanted nothing but the best for them. Now, again, I'm not saying that money and social status are negative things. What I'm saying is that the people who have the gigantic houses often have those houses because they work 70 hours a week and don't get to snuggle with their kids. The kids with the perfectly laundered clothes are the same ones who weren't allowed to play in the rain, dig to find bugs, or come within ten feet of finger paint. The ones who were pushed to be in the gifted class, on the high-level competitive teams, and extracurricular warriors, were many times suffering from internal stress and anxiety due to the pressure to keep up.

Comparing kids and families only results in negative feelings, your child's *and* your own. The self-doubt and constant questioning can absolutely rip you apart and destroy your mindset as a parent, and as a person. Studies show that approximately 1 in 6 Americans take antidepressants, and much of it can be traced back to one common question: Why can't I? Why can't I make more money? Why can't I be skinnier? Why can't I find a partner? Why can't I be more like... them? As parents, we subconsciously (and often times consciously) ask the same question. Why can't I have better communication with my kids? Why can't I have kids that are academically stronger? Why can't I have less stress in my house? The answer is that nobody has it perfect. Let me say that again. NOBODY has it perfect. At some point in his life, Gandhi probably uttered the phrase, "What the fuck" under his breath at his kids. Abraham Lincoln had to drink four score and seven beers just to make it through some days with his kids. Mother

80

Theresa even probably had dreams of getting in her car and driving to Arizona, befriending a thorny toad named Tony, and living somewhere in the desert where nobody would find her... she had kids right? I would assume that's why they call her "Mother?" Kidding. You get my overly embellished point though... it's difficult for us all, no matter how patient, forgiving, understanding, and loving we are. Recognize that you are flawsome: Awesome despite, and because of, your natural human flaws. If you are doing your best, then you can do no more. Be satisfied. Feel as though your cup is full, and appreciate all that your child is, not what other people's kids appear to be.

Children are extremely observant creatures. They pick up on what we do, what we say, what we don't say, how we look, how we react, and how we behave. They notice *everything*. If they start to get the feeling that they are being compared to another child, intentionally or unintentionally, they will pull back. It is easily observed in families with multiple children, where the younger child feels pressure to live up to the standard set by older sibling, regardless of ability and interest. It's easy to forget that every child is so uniquely different. Siblings are often polar opposites and have their own strengths and weaknesses. In my own experience with having twins, it never fails to amaze me how different my son and daughter can be, even though they shared the same DNA, womb, nutrients, parents, birthday, environment, attention, and education. My son is quiet, reserved, and cautious, while his twin sister is Hannibal reincarnate, riding through the Alps with her militarized pachyderms on the way to sack Rome and lay waste to Europe, stopping every so often so she can hike up her princess dress and go pee-pee in the potty.

In addition to being mindful not to compare our kids to those in other families, we must also be careful not to make comparisons to who we might "want our children to be." Perfect example of this is the middle-aged and overweight dad screaming at his son from the sidelines to "get up and shake it off," not because of his concern for his son, but because of his own deep seeded issues after blowing out his groin in college in a horrific intermural touch football incident, without which, he might've, maybe, kind of, gone pro. Our kids are not us. Here it is again. Our kids are NOT us. Whatever we were good at, whatever we have a passion for, whatever we wanted to be, whatever we aspired to? It means FUCK ALL to our kids. They're not us. They start from scratch and whatever they're into is THEIR thing. If your kid loves the same things that you love and you get to do it with them then I applaud you. That's awesome, I'll even come to his football game and high-five you when he scores a homerun or whatever, but it might not work out that way and you need to be good with that. If your son or daughter is into something that you have no interest in, try to understand that it's not about you. As long as they're not hurting themselves

83

or anyone else, you need to let them be themselves, and find themselves.

When it came time for my first son to attend pre-k at the elementary school that I teach at, we were excited to do the whole school shopping thing. He was our first child, so we spared no expense and went all out. New clothes, cool shoes, schnazzy folders, and his first real backpack. Does a three year old need a monogrammed leather bound weekly planner? Better throw it in the cart just to be safe. Top of the line graphing calculator? You're God damn right. Personal laminating machine? Let's pickup two. The last thing on the list was a lunchbox, so we searched online for the perfect one. A few minutes into looking at boyish dinosaur, robot, and construction themed containers, he said matter-of-factly that he wanted a My Little Pony lunchbox. He then calmly said, at 3 years old, that he "didn't care what other kids think, because I like ponies and that's all that matters." At that point I had two options. First, I could explain to him that colorful rainbow-shitting ponies were historically something a girl might choose and that no son of mine would be getting one of those, OR I could swallow my near-sighted pride and realize that he actually might be doing something more brave at three, than I had done all my life, and be o.k. with it. I chose the latter. Probably the most shocking thing about this story is not what he wanted, it was what happened as a result. And would you like to know what happened?! Nothing. He was three, and it turns out that three-year olds aren't really into ostracizing their peers just yet. None of the other kids made fun of him or even questioned it, it was just a part of who he was, and I was ok with that. Since then he's given up his interest in ponies and taken up the hobby of sniping his brother and sister with Nerf-guns, which somewhat crosses the line of not hurting himself or anyone else, but in the big picture I just want him to be happy with who he is, not with who I'd like him to be. I'm confident that the person he will become, will

85

eclipse my biggest hopes for who I would ever want him to be. He will be incredible, and unique, and amazing... and he will do it on his own terms, not mine. My point is, feed them, water them, nurture them, but let them grow... and maybe take a few minutes out to watch My Little Pony with them from time to time, it's actually pretty cool.

METAMORPHOSIS

At age 13, a boy by the name of Bill Clinton, worked his first job at an Arkansas supermarket bagging groceries and hosing down melons (not a metaphor) long before becoming our 42nd President and Commander in Chief. After growing up on a farm in Sweden and selling matchsticks to neighbors to help support his family, Ingvar Kamprad went on to open a trendy little furniture store known around the world as Ikea. In 1978, NBA superstar and arguably the best player to ever live, Michael Jordan was cut from his high school basketball team because the coach didn't think that he was cut out for basketball. The world's scholars once all agreed that the Earth must be the center of the Universe until a loony scientist named Copernicus came along, made fun of all of their moms, and then proceeded to prove that the universe was actually heliocentric. What does this all mean? That things, and people change.

If you're not convinced that time changes everything, a good place to find information on the topic would be the research and writings of the acclaimed scientist and his study of finch species of the Galapagos Islands, or the lyrics to any top-40 song on the radio right now, either one. Let's look at the latter example. Within only the past 50 years, what was deemed acceptable in music has gone from "I want to hold your hand" to "I want to wear your ass as a hat while I punch a child and dryhump a nun." On the Ed Sullivan Show in 1957, a 22-yr old Elvis Presley was only filmed from the waist up because tv censors were worried that he would menace the world's impressionable youth with his hypnotizing gyrations. These days, a kid staying home from school on any given day can flip on the tv and watch episodes of daytime talk shows featuring topics of social importance such as "Stop Pimping My Twin Sister" or "I Slept With My Girlfriends Brother" (both actual shows that aired.)

Nothing seems to be shocking anymore, because the world has changed so drastically in just a few short years. Entire species of flora and fauna have lived and gone extinct, transatlantic communication times have dropped from months to virtually instantly, humans have found ways to explore the far reaches of space and the crushing depths of the oceans, and hockey goalies finally got tired of taking frozen pucks to the dome and decided to swallow their pride (and probably some of their teeth) and start wearing face masks. Shit changes. Do you hear what I'm saying?

If Ice-T has gone from making songs such as "Cop Killer," to starring in the live film version of Marmaduke, it would stand to reason that your child will probably go through some periods of change and searching for their own identity too. Who they are at 8, 10, 17, or 21 will probably not be who they are when they are grown up, so don't worry too much. Your son doesn't like to read in his spare time? Maybe he will someday, and if he doesn't, then that's ok too. Daughter dyed her hair green and is listening to weird music? Your music was probably weird to your parents too, she's still a great kid and there's much worse she could be doing. Your child joined a cult and moved to Nebraska to go worship the great asparagus beings that are going to come down and transport us all to the next dimension? Ok, you might want to make some phone calls and get that one sorted out, but my point is that almost every kid goes through the process of finding themselves. It's part of life, and not to sound like my dad who walked 4

90

miles uphill to school each way without legs, but kids these days don't have it like we did.

It's really fucking hard being a kid now. They're facing challenges at a significantly earlier age than we did, and they're being forced to mature much earlier than what is developmentally appropriate. So many kids struggle with self-esteem, feelings of inadequacy, social pressures, and heightened expectations, and they're reaching out to grab onto whatever makes them feel valued and accepted.

When I was in 9th grade, my family was sitting at the dining room table having dinner together like we did every single night. That sounds very Beaver Cleaver-ish, but there weren't many "gee pops" or "gosh sons" being tossed around, it often times felt more like a formality. We ate together because that's what you were supposed to do. Conversation was kept generic and to a minimum while we filled our faces with meatloaf and, if we were lucky, tater tots. My grandfather would come up from the basement where he lived, and we would take bets on whether it would be his hearing aids or his teeth that he would forget that night. I usually put my money on teeth, because I learned that if you listened carefully as he was making his way up from the dungeon below, you could hear the faintly audible screech of feedback from his hearing aids that were inevitably turned up too loud. One night my older sister, who had been in the city with her friends for the day, most likely shopping for new Doc Martins and music that sounded as if it belonged in Russian interrogation rooms, called to let us know that her train was going to be late and that she would be home soon. Fortunately I was the one who answer the phone that night, partially because I knew I could make some of my brussel sprouts disappear in the kitchen garbage can on the way to the rotary phone that hung from the wall in our yellow kitchen. Overcome by excitement, my sister confided in me that she had gotten her nose pierced at some less than hygienic establishment on the Lower East Side, but she begged me to not tell my father because he had absolutely forbidden it just a few days before. Now, I'm not sure exactly what she thought would happen when she returned home with a nose ring. Maybe that my dad wouldn't notice? Maybe that he would suddenly fall in love with it and get one himself? I don't know. All I knew is that I had to go back to the dinner table, somehow contain myself, and bide my time until World War III came to an explosive start when my sister got home.

I'm not sure if it was the look of excitement on my face, or the sudden absence of brussel sprouts on my plate, but my dad instantly knew something was up. Trying not to make eye contact, I could see that he had put his fork down and was staring at me. His glare burned into the side of my head with the accuracy and concentration of a laser pointer taking down a low flying Cessna. Finally, after what seemed like forever, my father, a large intimidating man from Flatbush, Brooklyn, calmly asked, "did your sister get her nose pierced?" The only sound at the table was my mother dropping her fork and the screech from my grandfathers hearing aid. I tried to pretend like I had no idea what he was talking about without directly lying, which would've implicated me in the scandal and given my father someone to focus his fury on until my sister arrived home. I managed to play dumb long enough and creep towards my room, slowly so that my dad wouldn't sense my movement like the t-rex looking for the goat in that dinosaur movie. After reaching my sanctuary, I spent the next 45 minutes with my ear pressed against my door, waiting with sickened excitement to hear the front door of the house, announcing my sister's ill-advised return. As expected, tempers boiled over, voices were raised, doors were slammed, and somewhere in the distance I faintly heard the lonely song of a beluga whale calling to its pod.

It was many weeks before my father was able to get past the great nose ring fiasco of 1993, and I still swear that I heard my him whisper with his last dying breath, "tell your sister… that her nose ring… looked…….. ridiculous." What my dad didn't realize at the time, is that my sister's piercing didn't change her as a person. It changed her look, and maybe even the way some people viewed her, but she was still herself. Searching to find herself, not fully confident in which direction she should be heading, questioning who she was, but always herself. The nose ring was an expression of who she was at the time, but it didn't define her as a person or set in motion a series of events that would lead her to a hardened life of crime and double-streamed snot rockets. My sister went on to become a respected elementary school teacher, guidance counselor, girl scout troop leader, member of her church, and philanthropist. She changed from who she was, and is still in the process of changing into who she will be someday, which is what every person goes through whether they realize it or not.

It's not the first time I've mentioned this, but it bears repeating. We must love our children unconditionally for who they are, and not for who we want them to be. When you feel like you don't know how to get through to your child, like you don't know who they are anymore, or like you unsure about the person they've become, sometimes all they need is a lot of love and a little time. It takes time and effort for the ugly caterpillar to become the beautiful butterfly, but still we keep that chrysalis safe and wait for the day that it is ready to open.

CHERISH

Possibly the only thing that almost every parent would agree on, is that time goes by quickly. One day you're driving 20 mph in the right lane all the way home from the hospital for the first time with your bundle of joy wrapped up and triple buckled in, and next thing you know they're pulling out of the driving and heading off to college while you stand in the window waving and wishing that it was you going instead.

With kids, the days themselves don't seem short, and it can even often seem like your child might never actually go to bed, but when you look back at the last few years, months, or even weeks, it feels like it has gone by in a matter of seconds. They change so much and so quickly, both physically and mentally, that you might find yourself questioning, "who is this child? Where did my baby go? Why do they need a cell phone already?"

I remember talking with my sister when my twins were first born, and she made a comment that shocked me. Looking at the tiny newborns that I held in my tired arms, she told me that she barely remembered when her own kids were that small. In my mind, I wondered how she could possibly forget the smell of her baby's head, the way their lips quivered when they cried, or the small noises they made that were the cutest things you could ever hear, but I can honestly tell you that it's easy to forget. You'll remember much of it, but you'll forget the little things, which are the things that fill our heart up every day.

Whether times are good or bad, always be conscious of being in the moment. Appreciate the time you have and make the most of the experience while you still have it. Time, like this chapter, goes quickly, and you can never get back what you have already lost. Cherish every single moment.

PREPARE

Looking back, a reoccurring theme in my life has been one of unpreparedness. Beginning from a young age, I would do things like regularly showing up to Little League baseball games without my glove or bat, or even at times my team jersey. In high school, I realized halfway through the S.A.T., a test that is a big determining factor of your acceptance or lack-there-of into college, that I left my calculator at home and had to do all of the math formulas the long way and actually write them out. In college, I didn't realize that it was my scheduled day for my final oral presentation in my world history class, and I had to completely wing the entire thing in front of a crowded auditorium of people.

Since then, the feeling of being unprepared has come and gone in my life like that strange boyfriend your aunt has, who goes into the back room to sleep every Thanksgiving after dinner, and who's real name you're never completely sure of but everyone just calls him Uncle Johnny even though there's no way he can actually related to you. When I took the time to really sit down and do some self-reflecting, I came to the conclusion that my failure to prepare is deep seeded and mainly the result of the actions of two large and powerful groups in our country, the first being the Boy Scouts of America.

To be fair to the Boy Scout organization, maybe I should clarify that it's actually the fault of my parents, with the Boy Scouts being an unknowing third-party participant. You see, I was never a Boy Scout when I was growing up. None of my friends were. In fact, not a single person I knew in my neighborhood ever was. My parents just never asked if I was interested, and certainly never came out and suggested that I become a paratrooper or whatever you become after you build a park bench out of popsicles for old people to pee on outside of a retirement home. Rather than learning to put up a tent, tie 47 different kinds of knots, and becoming an expert in the secret not-so-secret finger salute, I was more concerned with running around in the street, scaling fences, hanging out in pizza parlors, and generally being a low-level degenerate hoople.

As a direct result of not becoming a Boy Scout, I was never exposed to their golden number one rule which is to "Always Be Prepared." I had no idea that being prepared was such a big deal! I thought I could just wake up, put my feet on the ground, and go about my day taking things as they come with no thought given to how I could help myself succeed or just make things easier on myself. I was too young to know back then, how could I possibly know? I couldn't just go down to the local den and sign myself up, I was a minor for Christ sake, and where do you even go about finding a den anyway. Every den I've even seen in pictures, looked to be miles away from Long Island, and most likely had bears in it. There was no Uber back then, so I couldn't just summon a driver from a magical device in my pocket who would then take me to the nearest den where I could take it upon myself to sign up to be a Boy Scout and improve my quality of life in the long run! And even if there was, who's to say that when you got to this hypothetical den it wasn't just your ordinary average run of the mill cave? Now you're suggesting that little kids have complete strangers pick them up and drive them to abandoned caves? All the knot tying in the world isn't going to help when you're on the side of a milk carton and your Uncle Johnny has left town again, know what I mean?

The second party who I hold completely responsible for my inability to prepare, is the National Weather Service, and the legions of weathermen and women around the world. Every morning on our local news broadcasts, neatly coiffed hair, pearly smiles, and meticulously applied fake tans distract us from the fact that these weatherpeople are only actually just taking a guess at what's really going to be transpiring that day. Their entire ruse is to convey an air of preparedness, when in actuality nobody's one hundred percent certain of tomorrow's weather until tomorrow actually gets here. It's one of the only professions that being completely wrong is just part of the job. What if doctors were allowed to just guess at why someone was dying, and there were no regulations and consequences if they were wrong? What if bus drivers starting skipping stops whenever they felt like it? What if restaurants let you look at a menu, and then just brought out cheese fries or pickle sticks regardless of what you ordered? With no ability to know what to expect, our society would crumble and revert back to a state of hunters, gatherers, and people who wear flip flops with jeans. Mass hysteria! What I'm saying is that in the weather business, it's

105

completely acceptable to be incorrect and unprepared, and watching those guys get it wrong every day and still driving home in a nicer car than your parents can be pretty enticing, so why even *try* to be prepared?!

Speaking as a veteran teacher at a public elementary school, I will be the first one to tell you that the school system will teach your child the basics of math, reading, science, and social studies, but will also leave out most of the life skills that your child will need to become a functioning member of society.

In the current time of high stakes state testing and gathering data rather than focusing on personal growth of the individual child, teachers simply don't have the time to concentrate on these critical skills that children so desperately need. Although teachers will seize every opportunity to capitalize on a teachable moment in school, many skills need to be taught at home. Let me be clear, I fully believe in the value of teachers, I mean I am one for goodness sake, but I do know from first hand experience that there's so much shit to get to and an extremely small amount of time to do it.

With teachers providing much of the academic knowledge in school, parents must also work to ensure that their child is prepared for "the real world." The buzz word in many school districts in the past few years has been "college and career ready." What this means is that the school system wants children to be able to continue on to higher education, graduate drowning in debt, and find a steady job making reasonable money that they can eventually put back into the school system when they get older and have kids, through a living nightmare known as the Book Fair, where all of your money goes to disappear in exchange for gummy erasers, holographic book marks, and unicorn posters. "You spent forty-seven dollars at the book fair and didn't get a *single* book?" Yes. Yes your child did, but the good news is that the erasers smell like raspberry!

107

Rather than "college and career ready," maybe we should be focusing our efforts on helping kids to become "life ready." We all know plenty of people who have gone to college and completely wasted their time, or others who have entered a career and simply hate their quality of life because all they do is spend their time working for a company that would replace them with a robot at the first opportunity they had. Is being prepared to sit in a cubicle really what we want for our children?

Every Monday in my class, I give my second and third graders a question that is meant to make them think. The goal is to not only to get their brain working after being off all weekend, but to spark discussions and get them talking and interacting with each other. Early in the school year, I asked them to take out a piece of paper and complete the sentence written on the board which was, "When I grow up, I want...." I could see the eyes light up and the imaginations start to run wild, as the kids quickly wrote down their answers without any hesitation. Pencils flew across the paper and the smell of friction burned erasers filled the room. After everyone finished, we took turns going around the classroom to share what had been written. Of the 18 students, 2 completed the sentence by writing, "I want to be (insert: a fireman, a veterinarian, the president, a manager at Denny's", etc.) The remaining 18 all gave answers such as an X-Box, a Ferrari, a horse, a mansion, a private jet, or something similarly tangible. With each answer, the kids got more and more excited over the idea of having whatever they could dream of, but my simple question to the class left them all surprised and speechless. I asked, "what about happiness? What about love? What about health? What about joy?"

The point I was trying to make to my class, was that just because we have certain things, it doesn't necessarily give our life fulfillment. There's a difference between joy and happiness. Happiness is

109

fleeting, while joy is a deeper feeling that becomes part of who you are. Happiness is the piece of chocolate cake that tastes good for a moment, but that may lead to regret soon after. Joy is the feeling of being complete. To be truly complete, we have to be prepared for life, not just academically, but socially, emotionally, and spiritually. Parents are the ones who can help the child become prepared. We have the gift of experience, wisdom, and patience, with which we can use to teach our children how to truly be prepared for whatever life throws at them.

Teaching is not solely the job of teachers, despite what the name would suggest. Parents must invest the time to teach our children everything we know and have learned throughout our time on this planet, from skills such as ironing and vacuuming, to life lessons like why we should respect our elders and the importance of listening. All too often parents send their children off to school expecting that they will return as perfectly functioning little humans who are ready to go out and conquer the world, while in reality teachers are scrambling to fit in a few short lessons a day and meet the demands of 20+ kids who have a truckload of different needs.

Like it or not, the moment you became a parent, you also became an educator, troop leader, role model, counselor, and collector of raspberry scented erasers. Do your best, and make sure you remind them to bring their calculator when they take their S.A.T., that shit is really friggin hard without one.

Perfectly Imperfect

LEAD

In the year 480 BC, Leonidas, the warrior king of the Greek city-state of Sparta, was killed in battle fighting against the mighty hoards of the Persian army at Thermopylae. He and roughly 300 of his men fought valiantly for days protecting a small mountain pass which gave thousands of their Greek allies a chance to escape to safety. Even when facing almost certain doom, the stories tell that the great Spartan leader remained in the front lines with his sword and spear, cutting down wave after wave of attacking enemies. Surviving until the last day of the onslaught, King Leonidas eventually succumbed to a rain of arrows that darkened the sky from Persian archers.

With his last breath, he fell where he fought, at the front of the Spartan army.

Although the story of the Spartans was popularized in an intense Hollywood movie, what many people don't realize is that Leonidas was in his early to mid-sixties at the time of his death. Rather than commanding his troops from the safety of his throne, he led his troops by example, quite literally all the way to the gates of hell. Facing such overwhelming numbers, each of the 300 Spartan warriors must have known that their story would surely end at Thermopylae, but I can assure you that with a leader like Leonidas, they had no second thoughts about being there until the end.

Although there are often days that we might *feel* as though we're up against thousands of Persian invaders hell-bent on our gruesome demise, luckily our job as parents isn't nearly that dangerous. Sure, we might step on our share of Legos, or take a scooter to the shin at times, but our clashes are more likely to end with mental wounds and emotional destruction.

No matter where our battlefields manifest, and especially through times of piece in the kingdom, we must lead as Leonidas did, by doing what we would expect to have done. If we want our children to be healthy, we must promote a healthy lifestyle and include them in things like exercise and appropriate eating choices. If we want our child to be kind, we have to first think about how kind we're being when we give the finger and unleash a chain of expletives at the distracted driver with the "My Child is an Honor Roll Student" bumper sticker.

It's open said that kids are like sponges, but I think it's more appropriate to compare them to dollar store lint brushes. Sponges pick up whatever they're exposed to, although if you need to clean a sponge you can just simply squeeze it out and start over, and kids aren't exactly like that. Dollar store lint rollers are made with some sort of industrial space-grade adhesive that is strong enough to once be used to fasten horses to their reins for pulling stagecoaches throughout the outlaw-riddled hills and plains of the post-Civil War American Midwest as they escaped from the buffalo riding coyote people. Like kids taking in their surroundings, the glue on dollar store lint rollers forms a bond that can only be broken by using complete disintegration at the molecular level. Once something gets stuck, it's never coming out. Much like the time my cat laid on a lint roller and had to spend the last 7 years of its life with it attached to its fur, my kids often bring up things that happened weeks, months, or even years earlier.

To this day, my oldest son remembers and feels the need to remind me about the *one* time I was pulled over when he was three, and given a substantial ticket for making a left turn through a red light (it was still yellow damnit!!) I try to look at it in a positive light and think that what he remembers most is not me accelerating my sweet minivan and power-sliding through the intersection, but the fact that I accepted responsibility, was respectful toward the police officer writing the ticket, and then did not make the same mistake again. The point is he remembers and has obviously thought about it, like kids do with countless other things that adults might see as insignificant.

We can't be perfect all of the time, but being conscious of the example we set is critical. One of the best things that we can do for our child is to show them that we are only human too. As parents, we have front row seats to watch our children grow up, but aren't they also watching us grow too? We never stop learning, growing, or searching for answers, and letting them see our own journey will make their own a lot less overwhelming.

Admit when you're wrong. Take responsibility for your actions. Apologize, and mean it, when you've done something wrong. Celebrate your successes. Set goals and challenge yourself in all areas of your life. Don't settle for less than you deserve. Work hard. Be passionate about something. Read books. Listen to great music. Have a thirst for knowledge. Show emotion openly and unapologetically. Tell people how you feel. Stand up for what you believe in. Know what you are worth. Love yourself and those close to you. Keep going when times are difficult. And if all else fails, pick up your sword and shield and head to Thermopylae, the Persian hordes will meet you there.

REFLECT

Walking into a bookstore or searching online, there are literally millions of resources under the broad umbrella of self-help. Books, websites, podcasts, seminars, support groups, motivational desk calendars. We couldn't begin to consume all of the information that is out there if we had a hundred lifetimes, but almost of all of it can be boiled down to one important grain of knowledge, which is to try to do better than you did yesterday.

Want to quit smoking? Start by smoking a few less cigarettes than yesterday. Want to get in shape? Exercise more and eat better than yesterday. Want to learn a foreign language? Practice more than

119

yesterday. Want to start a farm? Buy one more goat than you had yesterday. Simple.

All too often we get looking at the top of the mountain, thinking about how seemingly insurmountable the challenge is and how far we still need to climb, when we forget to look behind us and remember where we started and how far we've *already* come. So you're not at the top of the mountain right now, and newsflash, you won't be there tomorrow either, but by putting together a series of steps and continuously moving forward, you'll see progress.

There will always be factors that are out of our control, obstacles to slow us down and difficulties to make us think that we're not on the right path, but as long as we keep moving we'll always be making progress. The hard times don't last forever, like a storm that eventually runs out of rain, and it will make us appreciate the sun when we stick through it and finally see the clouds part.

By focusing on constantly improving ourselves, the relationship with our children, and the relationship with ourselves will grow to what we never could have imagined. We're going to make mistakes, we're human, but if we keep moving and make the decision that tomorrow will be a better day, then we're doing this parenting thing right. Our children are our most precious gift, and being a parent is the most important opportunity that we can ever be given. Of course we don't want to eff it up, but if you're reading this my guess is that there's no way that'll happen, simply because you care enough.

Ernest Hemingway once said, "There is nothing noble in being superior to your fellow man; true nobility is being superior to your former self." Similarly, psychologist Carl Rogers stated that, "The curious paradox is that when I accept myself just as I am, then I can change." Self- improvement is critical, and even though our destination may be unknown, we can always change our direction and start anew.

Our children come into this world with an unconditional love for us, as we naturally have for them. To them we are superheroes. They don't always see the stress and struggles that we deal with every day, but we deal with it for them. Our love is immeasurable, and no matter what happens, as long as that love remains, you're doing a great job.

You've got this parenting thing. You're doing an amazing job. Yes… you.

Perfectly Imperfect.

Perfectly Imperfect

About the author

Kent Lawlor grew up on Long Island before moving to Baltimore, and eventually settling in Ft. Lauderdale, Florida. In addition to writing, he is also a dedicated second/third grade teacher with a Master's degree in Montessori education. Kent has three children, including a set of twins, who keep him extremely busy and always laughing.

Made in the USA
Middletown, DE
26 March 2019